SQUARE
INCH
HOURS

SQUARE INCH HOURS

POEMS

SHEROD SANTOS

W. W. NORTON & COMPANY
Independent Publishers Since 1923
NEW YORK | LONDON

For information about special discounts for bulk
purchases, please contact W. W. Norton
Special Sales at specialsales@wwnorton.com
or 800-233-4830

Manufacturing by Berryville Graphics
Book design by JAM Design
Production manager: Lauren Abbate

ISBN 978-0-393-25498-3

W. W. Norton & Company, Inc.
500 Fifth Avenue, New York, N.Y. 10110
www.wwnorton.com

W. W. Norton & Company Ltd.
15 Carlisle Street, London W1D 3BS

1 2 3 4 5 6 7 8 9 0

CONTENTS

SECTION 1

A House on a Hill   15

SECTION 2

Square Inch Hours   21
   J.   21
   Without the Color Red   22
   Act One   23
   Her Hair Tied Back in Braids   24
   On the Lower Order of Seraphim   25
   A Door Left Open for the Moths   26
   Where Once a Small Branch Fell   27
   Out of the World There Passed a Soul   28
   [. . .]   29

SECTION 3

I Was at One Time Close to Home   33

SECTION 4

Life Among the Vanished   41
   Fellini Attended by Nuns   41
   Mother Courage   42

The Consolations of Philosophy   43

Pessoa   44

Zenobius the Rhetorician   45

Ovid on the Near North Side   46

A Feeling of *And*, a Feeling of *Or*   47

Overseen by a Sliding Glass Panel   48

I Went for a Walk in Winter   49

The Bicycle Rider   50

There Might've Been a Cellist in the Dining Hall   51

Time Is an Accident   52

Self-Portrait with Shaking Hands   53

Apart from a Few Stone Bridges   54

The Italic Gods   55

SECTION 5

The Window Above Superior   59

SECTION 6

From an Unlined Spiral Notebook   67

ACKNOWLEDGMENTS

Many of these pieces originally appeared in *The Gettysburg Review, Great River Review, Harvard Review, The Kenyon Review, The National Poetry Review, Ploughshares, Plume, Poem-a-Day* (Academy of American Poets), *Poet Lore, Raritan,* and *Shenandoah.*

SQUARE
INCH
HOURS

SECTION 1

A HOUSE ON A HILL

I have a house. There are rooms in the house. In one of those rooms I put on my clothes. In another I prepare my meals and eat at the counter with the radio on. In a third room there is an armchair, shelves of books on various subjects, a few in languages I don't understand, and a small wooden table where, more often than not, I sit for hours following the pen across the page.

•

There are alder trees in the window, but if I take one step to the right all I can see are the flowered curtains people before me left behind. In the harbor, always the same three vessels: a trawler, a barge, a cargo ship, its deck stacked with red and blue containers, one of them filled with refugees. When I don't go out for long periods of time, the drone of the pulp mill detaches itself and becomes a faint vibration in the floor. It's easy enough to forget the mill and to feel the sound as something within me, something that carries on in me like a second sign of life.

•

Like a highlight in the painting of an eye that makes the eye more real, the morning jogger appears, not to distract from but to heighten the house's isolation. Had she in passing glanced up the drive, I'm sure she wouldn't have seen it as anything more than a retreat for someone in a far-off town. A person in general, not a person in fact.

•

On my occasional trips into the village, it's not uncommon to encounter people I've seen before. Some nod as they pass, some pause long enough to exchange a few words, still others speak, regardless of what they speak about, as if passing on a secret they trust me to guard. In each case, I try to respond accordingly, "true to life," for I want nothing more than to mix with people in the customary ways; to know that, whatever the spirit of our meeting, we have that spirit in common.

•

I often get drunk in the evening, and when I don't I write, and when I write I'm in two places at once, for I've never been able, as the saying goes, to lose myself in my work. From time to time I take a break to walk outside and look at things from a different perspective. And from that perspective I often find some phrase that pleased me moments before displeases me now. On more than one occasion, that experience has caused me to laugh out loud. What an absurd way to live! Have I got nothing better to do than write down a word, then cross it out and write down another word in its place?

•

Getting out of bed in the morning, now and then I decide it's time to change my routine, not to do away with it altogether, for I take it as a given, but to momentarily reverse its spell. To put off shaving until nightfall, leave the morning paper on the steps, turn on all the lights in the house and keep them on all day. Sooner or later the desired sensation of taking my life in my own hands comes over me, and I resume my habits as before.

•

One afternoon someone comes to the door and says, "So, you're still in the land of the living." He has brought with him a bottle of wine. He's new to the house and sees its possibilities. He looks through the books on the shelves, turns on and off the table lamp, sits down in a chair and rubs its arms as if polishing the wood. Although he doesn't bother to introduce himself, he refers to the past in a manner that suggests we'd once been friends. I can't think of anything to say, nor does he appear to want me to, though the longer he stays the more impossible it seems, the idea that I'll ever ask him to go.

•

In the end we leave the house together. Though he doesn't say where we're going, we take his car and drive out into the countryside, which is filled with sunlight and broad sweeps of spreading pine. Perhaps all along my silence was simply the prelude to a conversation, for we begin to talk about nothing in particular, though the tone is one of complete agreement, of two people who, from opposing sides, arrive at the same conclusion. As if to affirm our common bond, he switches on the radio to a station that plays only popular songs, each one as familiar as the next. From time to time he sings along, from time to time he taps his fingers on the steering wheel. At some point it appears I fall asleep, for the next thing I know we're driving through the outskirts of a city. The road has widened from two lanes to four and all four lanes are full. The traffic slows, picks up, and slows again, though the city never seems to draw nearer. It's early in the evening. My hands, I notice, are trembling. And from a now overcast sky, a light rain begins to fall.

SECTION

2

SQUARE INCH HOURS

J.

The reminders of her on the book she left behind: the taped tear in the dust jacket, the neatly printed marginal notes, the dog-ears, check marks, underlinings (single and double), the phonetic spelling of Russian names on the inside of the back cover. Closing the book, I wonder if I have seen too much, more than she might've liked me to, more than I might've liked as well, for when she later asks me how I liked the book, I respond in purely literary terms. Though I go on pretending nothing beyond that interests me, I can't escape the feeling that I too have been marked and deciphered and underscored, that even my deepest secrets have been subject to her claims as a reader. But what if she'd read me incorrectly? Or worse, what if all along she'd only taken me literally, simply as I appeared to be?

Without the Color Red

The lunchtime crowd was filing in and the waiter's disapproving stare let me know that I was taking up space. His blue shirt was missing a button and the damp underarms appeared to be dyed. Days before, I saw his face in a nineteenth-century daguerreotype at the Chicago History Museum. He was lying on a sidewalk in a pool of blood and, according to the caption, he'd been beaten with a pipe at a workers' rally in Haymarket Square. A semicircle of men had gathered around him and, because the image took time to develop, they stood with fixed, inexpressive stares. At the center of the group, one of the men, who was wearing a hat, was holding a hat, the way magicians do, with the inside turned toward the camera, as if to prove the corpse is real.

Act One

Although a number of the cafeteria tables were empty, a man and woman stood near a wall beside a vitrine in which the few remaining sandwiches were lined up side by side. She was well along in her pregnancy, and he had a way of rising up onto the balls of his feet as if peering over a fence. But by sipping her soda through a straw, then using the straw to stab at a piece of ice, she managed to ignore him altogether. And yet, hoping beyond hope, he kept rising onto the balls of his feet, he kept peering over the fence.

Her Hair Tied Back in Braids

A sudden, audible yawn—her mouth so wide it doesn't appear to be part of her face—from a girl reading at the library table. Then just as abruptly she closes her mouth and scans the room with the quiet, cow-eyed gaze so admired by the Etruscan painters.

On the Lower Order of Seraphim

From the tarmac spanning the lakefront, a group of teenagers dove, flipped, jackknifed into the water. Two days later, as if memory had been caught out in a lie, at the same spot, at the same time of day, another group of teenagers waded through water not deep enough to swim. Having drifted apart from her friends, a light-haired girl appeared to search the shallows, her hands moving on the surface in the slow circular motions of someone polishing a lens. Given that the summer was just beginning, her back was a blotchy pink—perhaps the lotion hadn't been evenly applied?—and where the strap of her suit had slipped, a lurid band, like a surgical scar, bisected the curve of her shoulder.

A Door Left Open for the Moths

We argued. We sulked. She walked out in the morning and walked back in the afternoon. After an early evening nap, we tried to make nothing of it. I set up the outdoor table, she peeled potatoes and turnips for stew. If only for the sake of conversation, we decided after dinner to talk about the past. As if quoting a line from a poem she said, "I never thought it would come to this." Silence. Then we cleared the table and blew the votive candles out. Stars came after. And darkness cheeped like a tiny bird.

Where Once a Small Branch Fell

Across a lightless landscape, a passenger train travels past, its eight airless, earth-colored cars trailing a loosening plume of smoke that thins into vapor behind them. Idling at the crossroads, I can see the blank faces staring out at the winter fields whose dense oak and poplar woods (where I hunted squirrels as a boy) were long ago cut down. On her way home from the Catholic school, a thirteen-year-old girl was dragged into those woods, raped, burned with matches and strangled with an extension cord. When two years later the woods were cleared, the "crime scene" was cleared away with it, and the memorial the family maintained—a small wooden cross wound round with flowering plastic vines—disappeared as well.

Out of the World There Passed a Soul

The hour of my mother's funeral I spent clearing out her overgrown flowerbeds, down on my knees in the leaf rot, nutshells, tiny grains of sandlot sand spilling from the runoff gullies. The hot work was to do not feel what had to be done, not to go on asking, not to wonder anymore. Full from scraps I'd found at the back of the refrigerator, a mongrel dog lay curled on a stone and watched me work. It was Sunday. The telephone rang, then stopped, then rang again. By the end of the day I'd done what I could, so I swept the porch, switched on the outdoor safety lights and, locking the side gate behind me, walked away from a house where no one lived anymore.

[. . .]

Every evening at dockside, the same men in yellow oilskins step on and off their fishing boats. On one of those evenings, as the dog days were drawing to an end, one of the men accused another of stealing his traps, jabbing his finger in the direction of the sea, his cheeks red and swollen as if from blowing on a horn. On an overturned bucket in the boat, a transistor radio was playing a popular song, and the boy on board, gaff in hand, went about his business singing along. Interrupting himself, the accusing fisherman yelled at the boy to keep it down, and the boy in turn turned to me and asked me who I thought I was. If only I could say it ended there, but guided by the logic of cause and effect, a chain of events had already been set in motion. So I remained where I was, imagining this, imagining that, waiting for what was still to come.

SECTION

3

I WAS AT ONE TIME CLOSE TO HOME

I arrived early in the afternoon and, on the advice of the woman who checked me in, had lunch at a local restaurant. The walls were a dark mahogany against which open portholes framed a series of painted nautical scenes rooted in local lore. The coasters were shaped like a captain's wheel, a drawing on the scalloped tablemat pointed north through a spyglass to the whaling station the state shut down a century before. My first thought was, Mother would've liked it, but Mother is dead, her soul having slipped through a pinhole in the bedroom blinds with which in the last years of her life she'd banished all natural light.

·

I chose a table by the window and watched, pigeon-toed up by the backwash entering the harbor slips, the returning squid and albacore boats reverse against the piles, each one an image I perceived as an "event" and my watching it as an "activity." Almost as soon as I sat down, I regretted not buying a paper, not so much to keep informed as to distract myself from the traveler's sense that if I don't look now, something will be missed. Because, I supposed, a pebble was stuck in the sole of my shoe, moving my foot—which I soon found difficult *not* to do—was like skating on ice, the loops and cursives scrawling out beneath me. So thin the ice. And the hand that pressed against it from below.

.

Once the meal arrived I felt fortified by the day-to-day rituals of taking bread from a breadbasket, cutting into a piece of meat, tasting for salt and pepper. If someone had been with me, I might've made a toast and had my toast returned. But then, weren't all the diners "with me"? To those who were close I felt closest, yes, but to those on the other side of the room I felt an affinity as well. In fact, it wasn't all that hard to imagine pulling our tables together and having the meal delivered to us on serving platters we passed from one to the other. I could see myself, as everyone rose to make their goodbyes, patting the head of a child, taking the arm of an elderly woman, shaking hands with all the new friends I'd made.

.

After a long drizzly offshore fog, the sky finally cleared, and it went on clearing throughout the day, the sun getting brighter by the hour, seabirds circling like ashes in the air. And then, as if a second sun appeared in another quadrant of the sky, the heavy, flexing surface of the water radiated outward from a central flare, the widening rings overrunning the pier until it seemed that only shadows remained, holding the places for what was gone.

•

As if we shared in the same experience, people on the street kept pace with me, and I did my best to keep pace with them. When I made an effort to meet each glance, my gesture was returned in kind, and throughout the afternoon I went on responding to this, not that, going here, not there, trusting myself to fate. In the Shipman's Bar I basked in the secret knowledge that something was going to happen, that someone was going to arrive and, immediately, go away, or not go away, or stay and not go anywhere and never go away. Had the bartender engaged me in conversation, I would've shown great interest in whatever subject he raised, but how much more I would've liked to take the next step and buy a round of drinks, or pour my heart out to anyone close enough to hear.

•

In the early evening there were very few people on the streets— even the restaurants appeared half-empty—which was fine with me. Plenty, perhaps too much, had already happened, and I replayed in my mind the time I'd spent watching a pair of copulating flies on a windowsill, the book I'd read in a coffee shop about the bandit

Tiburcio Vásquez, the walk I'd taken at low tide to search among the rock pools for anemones. After such a long day of sensations, I not only felt exhausted, I also felt I'd lost the means to think coherently about anything. Even though it was early, I looked forward to the moment when I'd return to my room, put myself to bed and, in the slow rotation of the bedside fan, turn my back on my surroundings.

•

Sleep came and passed and in between a dream of her lying in bed while the caregiver, with the absurdly repetitive movements of someone rehearsing a play, dressed her naked body in the clothes she'd be cremated in. Rising earlier than usual, I went outside to get some air, but as soon as I closed the door I was struck by an irrepressible urge to break into a run. So I ran, and I kept on running, and I didn't stop until, unable to run any longer, I collapsed on the verge of an open field. The grasses blew from right to left. From right to left a contrail crossed so high overhead I couldn't see the plane it issued from. Birds, shadows, treetops, everything moved, one thing following another, all moved in the direction of the wind.

•

By the time I got back to my room I realized there was no point in staying on longer. The news reported that up and down the coast the weather was clear and would remain that way for the rest of the day. If I left by noon I'd be back in my apartment before dark, and it was there I knew that in a day or two I would try again, jotting down the intermittent notes, organizing notes into sentences, endlessly erasing and filling in. At the very least that was something to do—perhaps that was all there was to do—but surely that was not nothing. Surely it didn't end there.

SECTION

4

LIFE AMONG THE VANISHED

Fellini Attended by Nuns

The drugs he was administered left him comatose for hours on end, and in between, in moments of semiconsciousness, he floated through a realm of intense, horrifying visions: his room like the inside of a mouth; his head like a small good-luck egg, the kind one sees in bakery windows lying on a piece of tulle; the entire façade of the Palermo cathedral collapsing around his bed. Awake, he wondered if he was dying, and he wondered if he was dying from fear. But fear of what? That the film he was planning to make—*Il viaggio di G. Mastorna*, which he never made—exceeded his strength to do so. In time, the hallucinations were replaced by a greater fear: that things were only what they were. The telephone was a telephone, the bed was a bed, the door did what doors do. And no matter how hard he struggled, no matter how much he focused his attention, nothing was more than it was meant to be. And yet voices went on asking: "Would you like some paper?" "Can I bring you a pen?"

Mother Courage

To the trim, tethered sailboats in the marina, a madwoman at the end of the pier sang a song composed entirely of obscenities. The woman haunted Brecht for weeks, but each time he tried to write her into a scene he was stopped by the impression that, no matter how he staged her, her presence was more symbolic than real. Given his distaste for literary effects—"not even my imitators would stoop so low"—time and again he struck her out, crumpling the pages and tossing them into the fire, time and again she came back as before. Was she better suited for an opera, perhaps? Or a poem? Was she better left alone as an entry in his journal: *Early evening. Funeral bells. Madwoman raving at boats in the marina.*

The Consolations of Philosophy

In his college days, Nietzsche wrote nine autobiographical sketches in which he not only examined himself—"the dividuated individual"—but projected himself into a future where, in the Dottendorf Library Reading Room, he would read what he'd had to say about himself. By the time the future came round, the man who read the man he'd been was the very man he thought he'd be: "In the past four weeks, I have finally understood my own writings; not only that, I admire them."

Pessoa

At some point in his early twenties, the old-world Sensationist began
to speak, not *as* himself, but *for* himself, the great author of his
poems, Álvaro de Campos. And what was that sensation? "Of facing
myself left behind on the seat of a trolley."

Zenobius the Rhetorician

A travel magazine lists the charms of its far-flung off-season getaways: "Crowd-free, Stress-free, Snob-free." The getaways are then divided into "Seaside Romance, Mountain Adventure, Desert Escape." Above each destination, enormous stars are lifted into place by industrial cranes, and star-to-star the music of the spheres amplifies the candlelit terraces. Is there anything beyond our imagining, Praxilla? And if poems get written about lesser things—a soapstone bowl, the peelings of an orange, a braided horsehair ring—what are they in the face of all this?

Ovid on the Near North Side

Whether from willfulness or lethargy, each day he spent in the foreign city brought a growing detachment from the past, from anything, that is, that made the past accessible. At the same time, his life assumed the custom of necessity. Even morning walks along the river ended always at the kiosk where he'd buy his cigarettes and paper. Whatever small problems arose (though he wasn't bad-looking, women seemed to find him unappealing), he at least felt less and less obliged to think of himself as a Poet. The part in the hair of the bus driver, the palsied hand of the grocery clerk, the deep gouge, like a bullet hole, in his apartment door, those were the fugitive images that crossed his mind as he pondered the great work of his final years.

A FEELING OF *AND*, A FEELING OF *OR*

Mid-morning, mid-summer, the bedroom window raised, and where the screen intersects with the frame, a web of circular tensile silks radiating outward from the central lair where a yellow spiny-backed spider waits, its six thorn spurs protruding rose-like from the abdomen, its casing imprinted with a wax seal ring. Attached to the foundation lines, clusters of white cottony tufts—lures, I suppose, for insects—and suspended from a single thread, a much smaller egg-shaped spider swaying imperceptibly in the air: an image from childhood that reminds me of "childhood," a word that so often crosses my mind that it long ago ceased to mean anything other than a period of time when things occurred, not to *me* so much as *him*, all of them linked only by AND. As in the span of a single moment: the afternoon after the all-clear when the sun rose on a bloated, fly-stung pygmy goat in a gravel slough *he* crossed to wave to a woman with a Red Cross band on her arm. AND: the red pinball bumper cap ("5000 when lit") in a tented arcade on Brighton Pier when *he* was twelve.

OVERSEEN BY A SLIDING GLASS PANEL

Eye-level in the unlocked common room, a fireplace fire played in a loop on the television screen. It was difficult to say where the loop began, though the logs continued to burn, and the flames continued to rise. As if testing the heat of the fire, a woman (no more than a girl) reached out to touch the screen. A cell phone rang unanswered. An elderly man, whose face I didn't recognize, turned the pages of a magazine; across from him, tiny and archaic, an even older woman pressed the fingers of one hand to the corresponding fingers of the other. Out of consideration, no one looked at anyone directly but at everyone from the corner of an eye. Apart from that, we kept to ourselves. From a distance it might've appeared that we were there because we had nothing better to do, and nowhere better to do it, that nothing mattered less than the world outside. Even the artificial palm in the corner, even the attendant nodding at her station, even they conveyed the impression that, though we were present, we had thought our presence away—and, moreover, that we'd chosen to.

I WENT FOR A WALK IN WINTER

The snow didn't fall so much as blow past horizontally. People heading east leaned into it, people heading west leaned back, then one after another they disappeared, as in the fade-out of a movie screen. As if the world were reduced to the simplest natural law—that of erasure—a hotel doorman struggled to clear a sidewalk path that quickly filled in behind him. So, too, the hollow left behind on a bus stop bench. Above the entry to a corridor, a blue and yellow neon sign lit my side of the street. I felt my body pass through it, and I felt its colors pass through me, as though a mood had suddenly come and gone, leaving only a tremor behind.

After I returned to my apartment, I found it difficult to focus on anything; and when I switched on the television it took me a moment to realize that a movie in a foreign language was on, though what language that was I couldn't say. The uniforms of the soldiers locked in battle were likewise unfamiliar, and the frozen landscape provided no clue. Muskets were fired, swords were drawn, orders were shouted and, I assumed, carried out, for bodies continued to drop in numbers carnage alone explained. Somewhere offscreen, wagons were already being readied to haul away the dead, and this too I took in, less to imagine the event than foresee the end: the battlefield cleared, the blood covered over by ever-amassing drifts of snow.

THE BICYCLE RIDER

Already in the evening the day seemed longer than it was, though it also seemed more coherent, more cinematic, as if by some unspoken logic everything was finally falling into place, one image picking up where another left off, each in the natural order of things. A man stopped a woman walking toward him on the street then together they walked off in "her" direction. Walking in "his" direction, three adolescent girls approached a policeman to ask their way. Beneath the news ticker's digital scroll on the building behind them, three more girls posed for a photograph with their tongues sticking out. Having broken free of his father's hand, a small boy hurtled toward them, his delighted shriek like a rooster's crow, and his father's call like the hoot of an owl. Things went on occurring just that way until, while waiting at a crosswalk for the light to turn, I began to doubt the truth of my perceptions. To suspect that like some Hollywood film I'd been making up rather than experiencing them. To escape that impression, I turned around and hurried off in the opposite direction, rushing to outpace people in my lane, passing on the left then pulling back into line, like someone riding on a bike. Someone with no other purpose in mind than to get where he's going as fast as he can.

THERE MIGHT'VE BEEN A CELLIST
IN THE DINING HALL

As we walked through the ward, I was surprised to see how the community he moved in wasn't so different from the one he'd moved in when he was well. At least not in his mind, it wasn't. The old gestures of social nicety still came into play. He greeted other patients with a wave, paused to shake hands with the janitor, tipped a nurse with an imaginary coin. Gone were the Italian shoes, exchanged for Velcro sneakers, the expensive suits and ties, replaced by sweatpants and an undershirt. Half his face was unshaven, his hair appeared more cropped than cut, and yet—as if in this and this alone his connection to the past was real—his nails were beautifully manicured.

TIME IS AN ACCIDENT

Sitting in the park with a book that (finally) shed no light on the past, I began to move my lips as I read, focusing not on the meaning of the words, but on the syllables, cadences, shifts in tone. As if learning to read all over again, I traced the letters across the page, returning now and then to the beginning of a sentence and starting afresh. It wasn't until a church bell rang that I lifted my eyes from the page. A moment passed, as did a dog on a leash, the leash in the hand of an elderly woman who had grown too small for her clothes. She advanced at a rate so slow it seemed in defiance of the laws of nature, like a figure in a frieze who in mid-stride appears to the eye to move. As if lugging behind it the weight of the world, the dog continued to strain against the leash, tug aside to sniff at something in the grass, rise up onto its hind legs to bark at squirrels in the trees. All the while, the book lay open on my lap, my finger pressed to mark the spot where I'd left off when the church bell rang, though I couldn't have said what I'd been reading.

SELF-PORTRAIT WITH SHAKING HANDS

The Russian vendor I've bought the paper from for years asks if I am cold.

No.

Are you afraid?

No.

Why are you shaking?

Am I shaking?

What happened to you?

For a long time after I find myself searching for what had happened to me, stopping now and then to see if my hands are shaking, are *still* shaking, which in fact they are. A sequence of events interrupted when, from an open window, I hear a song I remember from my youth, though a few moments later I can't remember what song it was, only the pleasure of having heard it again.

APART FROM A FEW STONE BRIDGES

Half an hour outside the ancient city limits, down what was once a mill road and now a shortcut locals take to a highway in the north, lie the grounds of a ruined estate, its confines marked by boundary stones dense hummocky clumps of grass make difficult to see. In the turnaround, a marble bacchante, her life-size body balanced on a plinth, a castanet in her upraised hand, her eyes closed, or almost closed, in the pleasures of the dance. Except for the occasional passing car, sounds one would normally expect to hear, the natural and the man-made, don't rise above my footsteps on the gravel path. On the choked-off limbs of the orchard trees, vines that appear to have grown, not up, but down the trunks before taking root. The copper-colored underside of dead leaves, and at the tips of the branches, deformed clusters of terminal buds covered in fungus like an animal's pelt. All that I recorded twenty years ago—to what end I couldn't say, beyond a wish to renew my ties to the world—on the back of a rental car folder, near the sluggish waters of the Lys.

THE ITALIC GODS

In the back room of a secondhand bookshop on Printer's Row, I leafed through a stack of nineteenth-century topographic maps spread out on a table and weighted with a stone. I was the only customer in the store, and though he'd checked my bag when I entered, the desk clerk hardly glanced my way. Like the stone, his heavy head rested in the palm of his hand, the blackish-blue tattoo of a griffin rising off his knucklebones. One map charted Alexander's march across the Dardanelles into Asia, along the Lycean shore through the Great Sand Sea to the Siwa Oasis where an oracle declared him the Son of God. Half a life ago, I came across a Johann Platzer painting of Gordius's old wooden-wheeled cart (a kind still seen in Anatolia) where yoke and shaft are fastened by a knot made of cornel bark. More man than god, Alexander has raised his broadsword up to strike the knot, and fear is in the faces of those foreseeing what's to come.

The windowless room was damp and overheated, yet I was glad for its privacy, and I was grateful to the clerk who, as they say, turned a blind eye. Outside, dusk was settling and it had started to snow. Businesses were closing and the sidewalk was crowded with faces that were, by turns, kindly, expressionless, desperate, cruel and, as if each held up the homeless woman's cardboard sign—"I Am Like You"—no one bothered to be different than he was. I was in no hurry to get home, so I continued on beyond my subway stop and by the time I reached the Wells Street Bridge, the crowds had thinned to a handful of people. All along the railing, pole flags for the military dead hung slack above the river. When I closed my eyes, I could feel the water sliding past the wooden pilings, and when I opened them again, the streets were so quiet it seemed all the cars in the city had shut off. If this wasn't peace, it was nonetheless an image from which the experience of peace spilled over into the world. A moment in its own right, pointing toward nothing beyond itself, only it and what would become of it.

SECTION
5

THE WINDOW ABOVE SUPERIOR

An outdoor bench in the hospital gardens, the terrace bordered by waist-high, vase-shaped bushes. Because it was Sunday, the streets were empty and sounds not audible for the rest of the week were audible then. The opening and closing of a door. The voice of a man scolding his child. A moped stopping at the curb. Bird sounds, and not just city pigeons, but finches, chickadees, starlings, jays. The gardens weren't too crowded, the sunlight wasn't too bright, the air was neither too hot nor too cold. Though I observed them very carefully, the expressions on the faces of the people nearby were careful not to give anything away. To my left, the branch of a shade tree hollowed by insects still bore a few leaves, and where the forked trunk split, a plastic grocery bag was lodged like the nest of an animal or bird. And so the hour passed, each moment saved from a morning wasted in useless self-reflection, and by the time I went back inside, anything seemed possible, happiness as well, as long as my mind kept pace with whatever new sensations came my way.

•

On the wall behind her wingback chair, a painted canvas of Tuscan tiles, the brushstrokes varying from one square to the next, first left to right, then top to bottom, then left to right again. Though I expected it to be filled with tissues, the trash can beside me was empty, as was the acid green Lucite vase on her desk. It seemed wherever I rested my eyes I was reminded that I'd be talking to a stranger. As if I were a newcomer to my own emotions, the first thing she asked me was, "How do you feel?" I did my best to give her a thoughtful answer, but when I saw that she didn't note it on her legal pad, I began to revise, augment, elaborate on what I'd said. This went on until I was no longer sure what I was trying to say, as if my words had only confused my thoughts, and I felt the urge to ask if I could start over. Perhaps to encourage me to continue, she took up the narrative and played it back more or less in my own words, more or less repeating my emphases and pauses as she carried the monologue through to the moment where I left off. But why stop there? Since we already shared a point of view, why not push on to the conclusion? Instead, we arrived at a "natural stopping place." Pleased with the progress I was making, she stood and warmly extended her hand and I, in turn, received it (slavishly) in both of mine.

·

Having signed out earlier in the day, I bought apples at the farmers' market, a wedge of pie at the bakery, a newspaper at a stand. On my way to catch the crosstown bus, I stopped to watch as one by one a tower crane raised a rusted (or rust-colored) I-beam from a flat-bed up twenty-some stories to the roof of the new Maternity Wing.

The framing in of the final floor provided occasion for a topping-off party in the courtyard of the art museum across the way, a slate space where, each at a different angle, a number of bannered canvas tents were anchored to bags of sand. I took a seat on the ledge of a concrete flowerbed planted with rows of Chicago Brick wrapped in woolen sweater scraps and sprinkled with mustard seeds. In a few small patches of light, some of the seeds had started to sprout, and as I leaned in closer to examine them, a woman I took to be the artist arrived with a watering can. Because, I assumed, the project required the theoretical silence of nature, my polite inquiries were met with an unresponsive stare. Sympathetic as I am to the aesthetics of silence, to the childlike fantasy of escaping the material world of words, the cursive spray of her watering can and the fluent undulations that darkened the bricks gave rise to such intensity of feeling that even hours later, long after I'd stood and applauded the tedious speeches, I still bore the impression, the absurd, unshakable impression, that I'd been made the brunt of an elaborate joke. And the joke was part of the project.

•

As I was making my way back in the evening, I turned instead and wandered off between the high-rise apartments and village-like homes on the outskirts of the city center. I'd been trying not to think about anything, so I counted it a success when a tricycle abandoned in a gated playground didn't really interest me. When I didn't perceive as a personal threat the message taped to a door: KEEP YOUR DOG OUT! When a wrapper yellowed by egg yolk on the lid of a garbage can seemed no more significant than the can itself. As if sensing my lack of resolve, people coming toward me paid me no attention. Even those who happened to glance my way looked through me at something beyond. It wasn't that I had ceased to exist, it was as though through an act of will I'd detached myself from my surroundings. Were I an ancient Chinese poet, I might've found a bench beneath a flowering tree and composed a hymn of praise: *Pleased at last to leave the world behind.*

·

In my room that night I sat on the side of my bed, shoes untied, laces dangling above the floor. My shirt was unbuttoned and, like my shoes, it waited to be removed. I thought about turning the television on, but my roommate was sleeping and I didn't want to disturb him. He'd murmured something when I came in, though his words were addressed to someone in a dream. From time to time headlights from cars in the parking lot swept across the blinds. What at first I thought were monitors in the attendants' station down the hall turned out to be music from a radio in the room next door. As I listened to the music, my shoes began to move, following the rhythm of the song, the laces swaying freely, a feeling that traveled up my legs and into the trunk of my body. To open up even more space for it, I raised my hands above my head and closed my eyes; and I stayed that way until the song played through to its end.

SECTION
6

FROM AN UNLINED SPIRAL NOTEBOOK

A group of people gathered around a dead bat on the sidewalk, one with a cell phone taking pictures.

·

Someone on the subway platform shouts, "Get that stupid look off your face." And everyone's expression changes.

·

The moon rose earlier than the newspaper said.

·

As if silence were a way of revealing myself, I make a point of greeting everyone I encounter, even the man whose spike-collared mastiff lunges against its chain.

·

Was there a message for me on the crumpled page of a tear-off calendar caught between the drainpipe and the grate?

•

Small emotions, the great engine of my life.

•

To all outward appearances, she seems deeply hurt by his betrayal. But somewhere beneath those appearances, a suggestion that, having found a reason to leave him, she rejoices in being betrayed.

•

A feral cat approaches with its tail in the air.

•

A woman who walks with such lightness of spirit that after she passes I stagger beneath the weight of my body.

•

An enormous black bird—its head the size of an infant's fist with one mad eye glazed over with a cataract—perched on the branch of an overhanging tree.

•

A new idea turns out to be the same idea I wrote down weeks before, almost in the exact same words.

•

Take the alleyways, side streets, shortcuts (avoid being seen).

•

The child's habit of sitting quietly, minding her own business—all the while taking mental notes?

•

In the middle of the afternoon, I pull the blackout curtains shut, take my pills and lie down in the dark, which is darker for being light outside.

•

Curbside flowering lindens, like trees in a Chinese painting.

•

A couple who like pallbearers carry their lives through the department store.

•

The anesthetist yawns before releasing the serum sending me into oblivion.

•

Outdoor café: saucers of sugar cubes for British tourists.

•

A sudden dread of returning home because a week's worth of unopened mail is stacked on the kitchen table.

•

Getting up from a bench in the public gardens, I seem taller than I was before I sat down. Because people around me are shorter?

•

It takes just one unattended moment for an hour to pass.

•

From inside the diner, a sudden burst of laughter, as if a joke had been told, from a woman sitting alone staring at her grilled cheese sandwich.

•

No longer in pain, I continue to limp, me playing the part of my injured self.

•

Setting the book aside, it occurs to me that memoirs should all begin the same way, "First of all, forgive me."

•

As the helicopter passes, everyone's gaze turns heavenward.

•

How slowly the life seems to drain from her face as bite by bite her lipstick smudges away.

•

At some point in the evening it becomes clear to me that I spent the day refusing to do anything I'd planned to do in the morning.

•

In the middle of the argument she suddenly falls silent, as if she'd finally reasoned herself away.

•

He explains the funeral home's practice of donating leftover flowers to a nearby nursing home, "to bring the old folks a little cheer." But how terribly confused the flowers must be.

•

Vivid as an illuminated manuscript: graffiti on the side of an elevated train.

•

Coming back from the library, the sensation of being "accompanied," as though I were walking off to one side of myself.

•

Lying in bed, looking back on the day, nothing comes to mind but an old man in a blue apron.

•

After a successful morning of work, an afternoon spent washing dishes, sweeping the floor, taking newspapers to the recycling bin. Getting ready for tomorrow's work?

•

As if my body were inside my soul—a response to the new medication.

•

A woman who, having leapt back onto the sidewalk to avoid a speeding car, stands there trembling like a fly.

•

A decade after his death, the same dream: my father asleep on the sofa, his head on a pillow, a large black shoe on his chest.

•

By the time I get to the front of the line my fists are clenched.

•

Looking back in the rearview mirror at a car wreck I don't remember passing.

•

Free-floating spontaneous hostility, no, not me old man, a few apples from the back of the truck will do.

•

A religious thinker God can't forgive for all his talk about the human race.

•

A marigold raincoat hung from a nail in a ginkgo tree.

74